Hound Triptych

Book Editor: Krista Cox
Managing Editor: Krista Cox
Editorial Assistant: Kanika Lawton
Editorial Interns: Emma Goss, Marian Kohng, and Tassneem
    Abdulwahab
Colophon: This book is set in EB Garamond and Bellefair.

Cover Image: "Hound Triptych" by Genevieve Barbee-Turner
Cover Design: Kristen Camille Ton
Book Design: Krista Cox

Hound Triptych
Dani Janae

Acknowledgments

Anodyne Magazine: "Adoptee Log #3"

cart blanche magazine: "Ouroboros I"

Kitchen Table Poetry: "Ouroboros II"

RHINO Poetry: "the birthmother has expressive eyes"

Slushpile Magazine: "What Has Placed Its Hand on Your Skin?" under the title "separation, parts"

South Florida Poetry Journal: "Pushups"

SWIMM: "Search Engine Results" (in an earlier version)

Contents

for David and Dakota

There are many forms of love and affection, some people can spend their whole lives together without knowing each other's names. Naming is a difficult and time-consuming process; it concerns essences, and it means power. But on the wild nights who can call you home? Only the one who knows your name.

Jeanette Winterson, *Oranges Are Not the Only Fruit*

I let go of my claim on you.
It's a free world.

Frank Ocean

I

Hound Triptych

I

when i was born, i got on all fours,
and god beat me good. i could have
snarled, could have bared my teeth,
instead i widened my puppy-dog eyes,
brown like honey, and waited. it was easy
to fall for me. easy to fall in line.

II

i spent years learning the anatomy
of the cage. first the hard black floor, then
the nimble bars, thin as a toothpick. i was
so good i didn't even try to squeeze myself
out. i just wagged my little tail, gave a few
bowwows to the woman who saved me. i was
a good dog, i obeyed because my life depended
on it. i pissed where she told me to piss.
i chased sunlight until it made me sick. i was
a good dog. bow like heel, like surrender.

III

humans believe in the superiority of a spoken
language. an alphabet of letters and corresponding
sounds. in english, "a" sounds like "ay," and "c" sounds
like "sea." the animal world is not bound by such
limits. in spanish, "corazón" means heart, but in bird,
there is no need to speak it. the heart is understood,
is known, because it beats, because the bird can fly,
because the dog can bark, pant with a salivating

tongue. you can decide to only believe in the truth
of what can be spoken. the bird understands the figure-
eight path of its wings. the dog in the yard knows it's a dog.

i grew to hate the cage. through no miracle, i learned
to speak. the first word i learned was *bite*. bite as in to dig
in, to have a taste. something like release got hold
of my tongue, and i bit down, hard. i thrashed
it and didn't let go. i envisioned the bars of the cage
falling like icicles until they did. free, i spit blood.
free, i swallowed the damn thing whole. i forgot sweet
words and stood from my position. i wiped my mouth.

Sarah W—

In Western Pennsylvania tongue, you often hear
wurshed in place of *washed*, as in, "She *wurshed*
her hair in the kitchen sink, careful to detangle
the knots as they appeared like small mammals."

I say *washed.* I toss my mother's name like a pebble
into a lake, the syllables ripple in the water of my mouth,
hold tight to my molars, hiss at the tip of my tongue
forming bright foam as first it lifts, then falls, separates.
When I think of my mother, I think of Elizabeth Bishop:

The shooting stars in your black hair
in bright formation
are flocking where,
so straight, so soon?

I have held shooting stars in my hair since I was 10.
Adults told me they made me wise, I thought they made me
mothered. Which, perhaps, means the same thing. I can
only wonder about how my mother plaited her own hair
over her shoulders, twisting the black with shocks of gray

into neat, orderly ropes. One and two and three, over
and over, her fingers slipping through the slick and oiled strands,
muscles grown tired at the task. The strength it takes
to conform, to contain, to continue. In all my dreams, she braids.

On paper only, I am my mother's child. I bear her last initial
in documents from the courts. Documents w—urshed of their
defining data. My initials, BGW, written at the tops of pages
that ask *who is selfless enough to keep the girl?* I've lost them
now. At 21, I moved so much across the city, leaving pieces

of me in every apartment. I longed to be a breath in wind,
I held smoke between my fingers and never unclenched my jaw.
First they took the name you'd know me by. You must
remember, mother, because you were there. Lying

in the same hospital bed. I have lost so much. A mother,
a name, the book of Bishop poems I gave
to a lover that turned into a stranger before
my eyes. When I w—ursh my hair in the shower, I'm careful
not to lose the still explosions, the maps

of the galaxy, the glistening strands. I am careful
not to lose what I love. I keep it all so close. Sometimes
I go so long without w—urshing my hair
that the mammals become large and speak

in their own language. So long they commune
by moonlight and dance. Who am I
to disturb their liturgy
with not my hands, but the hands of my mother,
the knuckles like little red stars?

Parable

My mother taught me not to trust
alchemists. She turned her body from home
to hollow, the bone of it shocked
to whisper. Instead, I kept a shrine
of her name, the skull of a coyote,
snake skin. A monastic practice of
of keeping the hours sealed and pressed.

But when I had my first   drink
my drunk drivel made an
alphabet
all of it, dizzy-milk-kissed,
            it spoke and said
mercy, mercy

the oar of desire   clung to me

   took seed

Go Ask [   ]

In a history of lies, the first:
a statement of authenticity.

A language adopted like a sheath.

I was once teenage
I was once   call it:
              "user"

I read the Diary before I
even knew what it meant to be

blissed. bleeding. blabbered.

[]

Oh, the assumed tongue
of girl.

Mindless, preoccupied with boy
poetic where it doesn't
matter   what matters

is this:

in high school, I begged the girl
I loved to bless me with the drugs
she sold, she said

Dani, you are so
good, *it would*
hurt.

[]

My first drink
at 11
Thanksgiving.

By high school I was already
learning to fill the clear bottles
                with water

to leave my father's beers

alone.

To drink the organic red wine
        while the children slept
in the house not mine.

[]

Anonymity will save no girl

especially one made up
whole cloth.

To make up a girl
is easy

just name [boy]

just talk in flowers

just call your teachers dumb

just assume form
presto
voilà!

[]

The volta comes
in middle school

when I thought the world
was fixed against me, when I knew
the only way out was through eye
of bottle. tongue of newt.

Cast spell and call her made,

call her freed.

When my mom
        asked about the bottles
I blamed my father.

[]

To assume the form of girl

just never speak about
        the cruelty

let a man seal his name in

your mouth with a   kiss.

Let him tell you he loves you,
        let your mom beat you.

My name was never Alice
My name was never Anonymous,
but I saw a flash of her in my eye.
I felt it on my tongue when I brushed
my teeth   chewed gum

to release the liquor from the folds
                of my mouth.

The lie is the point.

It is easy to assume
that drugs will ruin a girl
                        more than being

a girl will ruin a girl.

Drum up some pristine white debutante
and watch her wither at the whisper of heroin.

[]

To misappropriate
the sound   of a girl's
        voice

say: [boy]

talk about excelling in algebra
talk about your mother and father
        dutifully
only do drugs on weekends
        until weekends aren't enough.

I was once
teenage
I was once
girl
I was once
user

I was never Alice. I was never Anonymous.
Everyone knew my secret, my shaky hands.
But I excelled at playing "girl"

thin, straight A's, college prospects.
I excelled at being
until the bottle
          took me on its lips

until I said *bliss*

a viper for a tongue

[]

bliss
blisssss
blisssssss
blisssssssssed
blessssssssssed

say a-men

          say a-nother

say your name

say

who are you?

Poem As Motherless

Every poem I write is
a private monument to you.
I write them everywhere:
an eyelash on the pillowcase,
the flowers gone dry

and brown in my apartment,
the water that scalds the temple
of my shoulders in the shower
or when I stop to ask the black coil
of my hair what animal it is.

In this way, I am still
a motherless child:
I name things, I covet the things
I name, all of my silences
translate to missing you.

I make long lists of places
we would have gone if you had just
kept me in your arms. You couldn't
bear it; who could blame you?
I do and find myself wicked.

In every poem, I turn and find
your hands in its belly—
the ghost of you in the volta.
Each line like a strand of your
hair, perfect and ending.

Ouroboros I

I have yet to meet a snake in South Carolina.
My brother tells me a story of his front yard,
a hole in the ground. His neighbor charges
over, reaches into the hole, and pulls out
a thrashing, venomous serpent. Something
moves in the air between them, something
becomes what it was always meant to be.

Ꝋ

Something becomes what it was always
meant to be. Here, in the garden: movement.
First, I touch myself at the bruise, form
a fist around it with my mouth, always going
toward my body, so that I can understand
the certain and cyclical nature of destruction.
Each exhale an execution, the making of a myth.

Ꝋ

Each exhale an execution, the making of a myth,
I turn to narrative and find myself hungry. When
I stopped eating, I first learned the word "deficit."
Then I learned patience, the wall of the stomach
hollowed from ache. In the nightmare, my throat
so full, breath cannot release. In the nightmare,
pulling and pulling pieces of myself from the hole.

A Birth Myth

My mother already knew the pain
of birth. On her 10th child, she mewled
like a cat, birthed a black swan, a mink,
a blue rabbit. My head coated
in mounds of hair, matted with her mucus
and blood. She hardly wept as they
wrestled my shoulders from her
opening, instead gave a floral sigh.

Wasn't I miracle, red-faced, screaming?
Wasn't I starlight? My tiny fists already
shocked into form. The contract:
no contact. I scowled in photographs.
All things lost to the womb, I left
my name curled like a twin inside
of her. Dead, muscular and nailed.
Syllables citizen the flesh.

Her little animal, I was passed
to pink hands, clucking tongues.
My mother crawled from the hospital
bed, wiped her vulva clean of me,
pulled the placenta like a trick.
The guttural slope of my cry hammered
the NICU open, my spine shivered
and curved around her absence.

Sutter Home Sonnet

There is confession in the bright breath
of your Moscato, the ceremony
of popping the cork, licking its woody stump.
I lap my tongue around the glass rim
as if I am playing a song. I am not
what you'd call a musician, nor am I
thirsty. I am, however, trembling. Your
pink against mine writes a frightful sunset.

A good wine has to be both healer and
assassin. To claim a red heart with its
shimmer, the shine far from free. I am not
angry with myself—the fight between my
hell and my life was too ghoulish. Somehow
the bottom shelf holds the most sincere ghosts.

Search Engine Results

My entire life, I have learned to subsist on love that was not
whole, that was piecemeal, that was not made for me to begin
with. That kind of love makes you think you were born

wrong, a villain invading the crib. My adoptive mom
did not love me in a way I could understand, so I learned to live
in the hollow. I learned to love the mother that birthed me,

loved what I made her: a quiet, bookish woman who played
piano. When she was not who I wanted, I learned to love
who she was. I searched any approximation of her name,

and learned to love the errors. Did you mean: *Sarah Walsh*?
Did you mean: *Sarah Welch*? I learned to love the woe.
I learned to love her demons. I learned to love her refuse.

Some loves are born of bone, they cannot be spoken,
only prized in the marrow, rich and pearlescent.
I've always loved my mother in defiance, against reason.

Do you understand? The weight we give daughters
to carry? Like a fruit tree, I spawn good children.
Each poem sparkling and juicy. It takes a new therapist

one session to name "abandonment." The search engine
says, did you mean: *absence*? Did you mean: *abscess*?
Did you mean: *abstract*? Did you mean: *abet*?

Abandoned, Abandoned, Let Me Sing My Song

Love don't live here anymore.
The ice caps melt, silver, a
blue plain, a swallow's shiver.

Call

When I get my hair cut, and the curls frame
my bountiful face, I think to myself: *you look
like orphan Annie.* Then, I want to call

the woman who raised me. I recall
school mornings between her knees,
hot comb ready on a stone.

She'd flatten and straighten my hair, then arrange
into orderly twists, adding barrettes
and ballies for color and weight. My hair

was the second most unruly part of me.
The first, dreaming all day of getting
free, emancipated as a cloudless sky.

My hair was so easily tamable: just add heat.
My spirit was restless. I planned
elaborate escapes, pictured myself wandering

the streets with a backpack full of clothes
and books. I didn't escape on the timeline I wanted.
I waited until 17, strained every

time I looked over my shoulder. Now
that I am gone, I want to call my mom just
to see what she'd say about my hair.

It is hard to live outside the tenor of her
voice, her vision of me still round and clear
as a doll, as real as something I could hold.

Ghazal For The Alcoholic

In the minutes before our dinner of bread
and milk, my family would ask me to say grace.

I knew a simple prayer, "God is great, God is good..."
We thanked Him for our food which in His infinite grace

He bestowed upon us. There was a great room in our
house filled with bottles of clear liquor where I found grace

and a clean drunk. Just twelve and ravenous,
my fingers—tall and primed—would grace

each bottle, lingering at the tequila. I wanted the worm
to bless me, swim down my throat with the grace

of a dancer. Livening the folds of my stomach
with its thrashing fervor. When I say "grace"

I don't mean the myth of beauty, I mean the elegance
of a woman, her neck adorned with her neck. I mean grace

as in God watched me get drunk through adolescence
and never told a soul—that kind of grace.

Sometimes the only way we survive is to phone it in,
to get off our knees and say a grace

that is bare, merely nursery rhyme.
When I talk about grace

I mean this language, my God, how it named me,
after years of silence and enduring, words now grace

the page, standing like lighthouses, like they aren't afraid
of falling short of grace.

On Paradise

In all the days that paradise
was built, it fell within an hour at the grace
of a fruit. Any alcoholic worth their weight

can tell you something of heaven.
I, wine drunk, would walk through
my neighborhood, stopping to piss

in the cover of bushes, convincing
myself this would help them grow.
I quit my job on a whim,

skipped rent and spent golden hours
watching my oregano flower. Bees
are drunks too, their fuzzy lolling.

Together we would sip our nectars,
turn spirits into afternoons gone.
It was heaven to wake up to the rest

of a warm beer, wash down the funk
of my mouth with its briny heat.
The pantry dry and wrecked with moths.

The rest of my money gone to a good day
as sun wrestled color into my wintered skin.
For as long as I can remember

we have blamed Eve when the ache
for an apple was greater than anything God
had promised. I have had only one beloved.

There was paradise in my goblet, a worship
in every sip, my throat lined with cool
wine. My song was this, simple and bare,

my hands forming forever around a glass.
I lost everything, my heaven, the last call
of a friend who has had enough.

I was the worst of a bad evening, was the ash
of a cigarette, was the mud caked in the grooves
of a shoe, was the stale light above the kitchen sink.

What Said The Apple

Abandoned, what, if anything, could be said?
Having tried to open its mouth and found no
mouth, having lived through the horror of its
descent toward earth, naked, bare as Eve.
Everything, everything comes up with dirt
on its hands. Still in the black shadow
of the tree, oxygen bore its horned breath
into the flesh, battering the crisp red skin
to a sunken bronze. Come carrion beetle,
funk-driven, burrowing through decay
toward sweeter stink. What could be said?
You survive a fall from heaven to sit at the root.

Things I Shouldn't Say

When the investigator tells me of my birth
mother's criminal record, I can only
think of the house I grew up in.

I can count on one hand the times
I had to call the police because my father
turned one of my brothers blue.

The one time I wasn't instantly
convinced to call off the cops,
two officers came in uniform

to the door. I told them everything
was fine, my hand gripping the frame.
The reflection of their badges glinting

in my wet eyes. That's the story of how
I learned to lie. The story they tell me
about my birth mother, how my life was better

without her, tastes like bad
medicine. Pale and syrupy, meant
to placate. I lied better than anyone,

lies shining in my mouth like veneers.
Lined up like houses in a suburb. Identical
in the way that makes your skin crawl.

A Colonial Project

I called the bluff. I swallowed the pills.
I told myself if I didn't kill me, mom would
kill me. So, I took the razor blade, stood

at the bridge. In countries torn apart by war
and genocide, in families where food was scarce
and drugs were a balm, children made motherless

were left to be raised by white mommies.
I was born in this country of warmongers.
They took me away from my mother,

sealed the records. My white mommy taught me
the word "merciless." I was told I should be
grateful. My white mommy showed me

the right way to slit a wrist, said I was too dumb
to know how to die. Her ire like fine fuzz over a peach.
Rage glossed the gaze of her red-rimmed eyes.

They made an industry of the lost. They took
the bereaved, estranged them from their
bereavement, then made them change their names.

In Korea, after the war, children were stolen
from families that had reported them missing,
shipped off to the land of "better lives."

China lays its international adoption program
to rest. People grieve. People covet what they cannot
reach. My mom told me she adopted

more children because she was lonely. Lonely.
I grew up in a house bustling with babies
and I wrestled with lonesome everyday.

Oh what they built on the backs of us.
Billion dollar setup. They told me to be grateful
for the taste of my blood in my own mouth.

Corvus Corax
for K.

I'm going the way of the raven:
screaming. Covered in night.
Eyes so beaded black I need
to wrestle them straight. I recognize

the face in the mirror: mother.
I say *mother* in a human voice
then shoot into the sky, circle
the mulberry tree where smaller

birds cower. Everything about me
so shrouded in darkness, I cower
too. Like a bigger, badder shadow
cast over the caul. Mother. Nobody

knows it better. I laugh in a human
voice, smile and flash my tongue.
I make a meal of anything walking—
berries and stone fruit, even carrion.

In a human voice, I beg, *show me*.
But every desire has to grow up,
sprout wings, make a life of its own.
Decade after decade, crying out

each time I open my beak.
After, the echo. The wilderness of
my making, feathered. Eyes bobble
in the head pretty as pearls.

How To Perform a Self Breast Exam

Use the pads of your fingers.
Use the pads, not the tips,
of your three middle fingers to feel
the breast tissue with light pressure.

You can stand or sit in a chair, but
it's important to feel your breast with opposing
hands. Right hand, left breast. Left hand,
right breast. Moving now, with firm pressure.

The women of my family
died and died and died, all before
65. If my mother is still alive, she'd be
in her 70s, breaking or bucking the trend

like a wave breaks over the shore.
I love my breasts like I love my mother,
as a part of me, something to hold on to
for warmth, or when I am drifting away.

In circles, move your fingers. In short
circles around the flesh, inch
closer to the nipple. Feel
for noticeable lumps, abnormalities

in the tissue. You can press in wedge-
shaped movements from outer to inner
breast, or up and down across each one.
Search for changes in color or texture.

My mother has always been a part
of me, even as we exist two strangers.
When they run my blood for the cancer
gene, a part of me prays I have it, so I can feel

a part of her too. Another woman
in a long line of women with my blood
who barely graced this earth, leaving
like a lover would, still pressed against me.

You must raise your hand above
your head, place the palm of your hand against
your skull, as if you're relaxing on a far-
away beach, not pressing circles

into each breast. Calm, steady breath.
Make sure you keep breathing,
pay attention to anything, everything.
Nothing is too small to go unnoticed.

I examine myself at night, as I lie
in the cold dark, nipples hard
in the cool air. I notice everything.
I know what I am looking for. My blood

shows no gene, but the results say risk
is still high. My reward for being
my mother's child. An early death, a hard life.
Two breasts, magnificent and full as moons.

Feral

Like clockwork, the sun is
intercepted by longing: terse, yet
feminine. If all the children abandoned
to homes or churches stood together,
we would make a jagged robe. Non-
functional, but pretty, worn out
of a need to be wanted in whole.

a day goes like this:

fire, a moon interlude, lukewarm water, cold tea,
the color rose, clutching the fat perched
above my vulva like a roof, salt,
hours of hush, typing against migraine,
joints pleading for air, the harmony
of beasts, a prayer for my mother's life,
a sovereign cat, melancholy,
a dessert on an unwed plate.

You've Got an Enemy in Pennsylvania

On a call, a friend says something about being
"born to the state." I'm on a quest for my
birth certificate, the original one, the one
that holds my parents' names. There's a record

of us together in an office some-
where in the state capitol. The last piece
of evidence that we were once an us.
My first name, emblem of a girl

long gone, a placard for the dead, a title
for all my lives. Some registrar in the PA
State Department of Health, Vital Records
Division is now my enemy. She says they did

not receive my paperwork, and I want to cry.
At the end of the day I'm just a girl who wants
her mother. It's all so funny. To be this grown
and still yearn for her, hold her name

in my mouth like an egg. Later, I call
the post office here in South Carolina
and the line rings and rings and rings.
Maybe I've got enemies all across this great

nation. One enemy for every version I've been.
What you can make of an enemy is a cold, hard tomb.
I tell myself to give up everyday, but here I am,
paper in hand, the slope of each vowel begging to be seen.

Stella Rosa Sonnet

Sweet as summer in the backyard, summer
thin as a waistline, dill in the garden,
silky cilantro. Thyme. Guests ashing their
cigarettes against earthenware pots.
Sparkling, like sunlight. Or, better yet, sun-
dappled. Yes, like a cooing baby. Sun
shining through fingers lain over the brow
to shield the smile. Gnats swimming in a glass.

My last ten dollars. My last ten dollars.
Stella Rosa, sugar-laden, dark and
cloying as night wrapped around a waistline.
The hips sunk inward, the chalice, the bone
sharp as a knife. Potatoes sprouting green
eyes, green eyes shifting in the black pantry.

II

Adoptee Log #1

In a text, a friend says that to avoid abandonment,
she imposes a logic where she has more control
over how others treat her. Because, if you can
convince someone to treat you better, you might
also convince them not to leave you. Everything

is about control. When I was young, bulimia wracked
my body. I hated the surplus of my thighs, so I burned
and slashed them every night. Held steel
to a flame and branded the skin there. Not yet 18,
I couldn't do anything but go to school and count

my calories, eat at a deficit. Run and run to burn
the intake off. Adults told me I looked good, that I
was wise beyond my years, more mature than my peers.
All I wanted was my mother. Pathetic. Like a baby
whining in its bassinet. I pined, I craved.

When I left home, I was still whistle-thin. When I
started having sex, I learned to leave my body, lean
above the woman and whisper aching things into her
mouth. I didn't let her touch me. I garnered a reputation.
When my mother said she didn't want me

for the second time, I turned to drugs. Control. Control,
and Captain Morgan. Ran to the liquor store on my
21st birthday, arrived right as the doors opened. Jed, who
brought me spiced rum. The beautiful pills. Then,
mimosas with breakfast. Rosé with lunch.

Red wine with dinner. Control, control, control. If you
could be a songbird why would you be a beast? Would you rather
be a monk or a dog in heat? These decisions are easy
if you think they're yours to make. See, what my mother had
was opportunity. All I had was desire. See, you thought I wouldn't

say beast. Oh, ache. The illusion of control. My mother was all
I could ever want. Some wants can devil your blood,
cover you whole. I learned the power of narrative.
See, when I said gaunt, I meant *garish*. When I said whistle,
I meant *worship*. When I said desire, I meant to say *destiny*.

Adoptee Log #2

The adoption was closed as if, like an animal,
it would lunge at you if you opened the doors.

For years, I don't open the windows. I don't open
the doors. I keep my life closed, delicate. It appeases

the mystique. The paperwork must be sent through
the mail, must be signed and filled out in pen.

I am seeking to open something that has long been
locked. The deadened rattle of metal. The whistle

note of the lock as it eases out of its position.
The website says processing takes 45 days. So, in 45 days

I *may or may not* receive my birth certificate.
I may or may not shudder as the wood moans, the dust

kicks up at my feet. The wind cutting and frigid. The heavy
door made up of years and years. Whatever waltzes from

behind it is mine. My mother, my grief, the musk
of a thing that has been waiting a decade to be loosed.

Adoptee Log #3

Because of the way the woman who raised me
talked about my brothers and I, I thought
that in orphanages, the children were in cages
and you could walk up and down an aisle and pick

the one you wanted like you would a dog.
I thought this for years. *I saved you*, she would
say when I asked about my mother, when she
perceived a lack of gratitude. *I saved you.*

Other times, she would tell me she had many
children to choose from, but I was so broken,
she decided to pick me. *I needed her*, she'd say.
I watch her stalk the aisles of the pound,

dragging her fingers along the bars, pointing,
saying "that one" as she met my sad brown eyes.
Years later, when my lover would tell me no one
else was equipped to love me but her,

I conjure up the image of the cage. Me inside
waiting to be saved. Me, so utterly pathetic,
so despaired, that a white woman need come to
my rescue, captivated by the golden uncertainty

in my eyes. In Manhattan, after her haircut, my lover said
I hadn't looked at her with desire in months, spilled
"I love yous" without intention. Again, the image
of the cage. My sallow face on the other side

of the bars. When I left her, her face was walled,
stern, as if she was certain I'd made a mistake.
Her eyes were cold as November, iced and sharp
like a blade that could cut me if and when

she blinked. To unlearn the narrative of the dog,
I stood up from all fours. I came to know
my mouth, the curve of my wicked spine.
I stopped howling at any sound at the door.

Adoptee Log #4

Jeanette Winterson says that adopted children are self-invented, that there is a void at the center of our story. A bomb in the womb. If you crawl into that void you'll find it has hair, teeth. You'll find your body rising and falling with its every breath, slick with its warmth.

A bomb in the womb:
Boom.

Sorry, I meant:
Born.

Adoptee Log #5

I'm sorry she hit you, my friend says.
We talk for two hours one afternoon,
and I tell her the woman

who raised me often hit me when
I asked about my mother. It was
always the same, always sudden.

I'm your real mother. She'd say,
cursing my imagination, my
will to picture a new life. In a talk

with my mentor, I again give in to
confession. I tell her the woman
who raised me took my early

journals and burned them. I had said
too much about wanting to die.
Said too much about rage

and revenge, two sisters that
grew up in the same house,
dressed in the same gaudy clothes.

When my friend returned to China,
she didn't look for her mother.
I picture her wandering streets

illuminated by gold light, eating,
drinking, remembering her *once
was.* Feeling the spark of connection.

I think about mom's hands, how she
beat me when I was terrified, when I
stuttered and couldn't meet her gaze.

For years, I thought anyone could hit
me. Teachers, bosses, authority figures
in general. When I failed a test, missed

a mark, I imagined a palm flying at
my face. Sometimes my cheek flares
with a phantom strike. The skin taut, red.

Adoptee Log #6

When I was young and still living
in Pittsburgh, I walked the streets of East
Liberty, my neighborhood, on the way
to the library. My shoulders huddled

upward at the chill. My lean legs
strode long and confident against asphalt.
A man, silver hair on dark skin, stared
me down. He chuckled to himself, shook

his head, and said "Damn, you look just like
your mother." Somewhere there is an
album of photos with my face in it.
Supple cheeks and a mean scowl.

Eyes like dinner plates. A crown of brown
tufts collected under a pink headband.
And as I grew, my features only became
more stunning: the swell of my lips pursed

into a pout. Ears like coins stuck
to my head. My mother's face remained
listless orbs dancing in the light.
A meal of incomprehensibility.

The man, probably mistaken or high,
walked on. For the rest of the day,
I saw my mother's face clearly.
Her teacup lips and dinner plate eyes.

Graying hair, the shock of the nose
as it descends down the center. Somewhere
real, there is a picture of her in a photo
album I cannot access with my hands.

Adoptee Log #7

I keep telling everyone, "I don't want her
to want to be my mom," that I just have
questions I have to ask for my health.

When I talk to my therapist, she says
it is okay for me to need my mother.
Like most people, I have wanted love all

my life. Pursued it like a hound. Gave my
body, abandoned my soul in pursuit of love.
And so I have betrayed my tenderness—

when I looked under stones for love and found
obsession. I am learning to forgive myself.
Because I was dogged, because I was hungry.

But it doesn't make any difference
now. I could beat myself raw and still not
feel the sting of penance. After the talk

with my therapist, I take a long walk and listen
to the shimmer of ocher leaves beneath my feet,
their noise like rattlers guarding the bite.

I walk and walk, searching for a way back
to truth, a tongue that can't form around a lie.
In the tea-dark night, wanting for nothing but sugar.

Adoptee Log #8

It's the holidays. I'm not feeling
like Christmas. My cheeks are rosy from the cold
and the sweat. It's hot in the post office,
a crisp chill swirls outside. I have on a white

coat that makes me look rich. Could anything
be more heartbreaking than this? Me, sweating,
hands like branches in autumn, reaching
desperately toward my mother. Only her first

name on the form. The only thing I have. I pray
to God. My wallet drops from my shaking hands.
All pieces of my identity displaced, that plainly.
I don't even know if I did it right. I just want

to leave the damn building. For the 45 days
to be up. To finally have my birth certificate,
my name scrawled in barely legible ink on stiff
paper. I can't shake the feeling that she's

dead and all my trembling is for naught. Wouldn't
it be kind-of funny if she were? If I sweat through
a sherpa jacket just to find her obituary when I
search her name? Forgive my macabre sense

of wonder. Forgive me, forgive all of me.
I hope my mother is alive so she can forgive
me. The woman I made her in my mind, the record
of her sins emblazoned here on my tongue.

Adoptee Log #9

When Jessie smashed the snake's head
with the blade of the oar, I thought
My God, somebody loves me.
All the days away at Christian girls'

camp, the fishhook in my thigh, her
name swirling in my mouth like blood,
a bitten tongue. When I came out,
all the adults wanted to ask about sex,

but I was 11, and all I wanted was
kindness. Love like hot sand under
my feet, cooling my soles in the murky
water. My mom asked, "What do two

girls even do?" and I shrugged in
the passenger seat of the car. It was
all anyone could whisper about
for weeks. When Jessie broke the skull

of the snake, I knew care. She didn't
want me to get bitten. She screamed, "Die!"
as the sun rolled over her shoulders
like a cape. My young, innocent desire.

I looked up at her and grinned. Her
smile met me where God could only
hope to reach. Let them call it a sin.
I was in love. The snake sank into

the waves. When I got home, I asked
about my mother again, and mom
reached around to punch me
in the face. Chasing love, I only got

the knuckle side of her hand.
To this day, she has never met any
woman I have adored. It is too
dangerous, my heart too ripe.

☼

A video says: *you must
decenter your mother.*
It's another rainy morning, and for
days and days, the mail is late.

I'm trudging to the mailbox just to run
my ice cold palm over its empty insides.
You must decenter your mother.
I scoff. Throw my phone under sheets.

My therapist says to make friends
with heartbreak, and adoption
is the biggest heartbreak I have ever
known. The admission scalds me,

I am tethered to the shock of it.
I go back to my mother's name on
paper, the image of the letter online.
The last name: W—. I search

"Sarah W—" and find first
an obituary. My mouth floods
with the taste of acid. I grimace
against it, tell myself I am wrong,

close the tab, and reopen it. I tell
friends that I am learning about surrender.
In learning, I breathe out, inhale an icy
wind, say, "Let this go," but it's like

a fish hook to the thigh: it won't be loosed.
I tell myself, the better part of surrender is
the surrender. Please, let go let go let go.
God, I am only so patient. Let me lose this

too. I am only so promised to this earth,
let loose. I say rescue. I say resolve, release.
I curse myself for not meditating after
one thousand days of transcendence.

I ask what will have to die to save
me from myself. The pattern
of destruction carved into me with fist
after fist, choking on my own bitter.

○

You must decenter your mother.
At night, I remember Jessie again.
Watching her from behind, doing
most of the rowing as the grass rose

green and sharp around us. I don't
recall what we said to each other,
but I remember her short brown hair,
just above her shoulders, wrapping

around her head to keep the buzzing
of mosquitoes at bay. What I want is
not always what I want, but a second
thing—a need in an overcoat.

When I say I want love, I mean I need
to be cared for. Losing my mother
was the long grief. When she left
me, I turned away from desire.

Turned into the escape, evasion
like a dance that is measured and
chaotic. My mother, at the center
of my world, collapsed it. I curled

back on my life like a serpent.
You must decenter your mother.
The grass is high and emerald.
Jessie is somewhere not thinking

of me. But that day, in the canoe,
the oar. The blade rising into a blue
sky, coming down with force against
a living thing. A flame lit within me.

Adoptee Log #10

All my fear for this.
My mother is alive
and well. My mother
is dead and gone.
Will the truth differ?
Will the truth unclench
my jaw, my fists?
Mother, I let go
of my claim on you.
I give you back to
silence, to anonymity,
I let you be a traveler
among thieves. Thief
that I am. My tears
selfish and in vain.
I let you pass me by
again and again and
again. I let you die in
peace, never knowing
me. Baby Girl W,
Betsy, Dani, whatever
name they call me by.
I'm full of tiny prayers
and foolish desires.
I'm full of cells that
look like yours. Can
you blame me for
being 18 and believing
you could free me?
Sarah, no other
mother has
loved me. Sarah, is

it true? Your kind,
expressive eyes.
Sarah, can it be?
Did you want
the best for my life?
I cry knowing that
you could *change* me.
Loving you has *changed*
me. Is it selfish, is it
cruel? Who is to say?
I'm still a girl. Or
I'm 32 years old.
Will the truth
unravel us both?
Will the tears on
my face still look
unbecoming?
Will my name
ring cold in your
mouth, its
syllables foreign
and unwelcome?

Go Ask —

Red, wound me.
Vermillion as a
vodka cranberry,

what you want from desire
        is not desire, sticky,
            wanton. Greedy mouth,

            there is a lesson to be had
at the bar, swirling in bisexual
light, gritting your   teeth against

morning. *Who are you*
if not the spinning girl
        pushing the moon up

the mountain with her head?
Who are you if not
                sullen debutante

slurring her words in the mirror
at a party? Colliding at break-
neck speed toward dark.

—

Water collects:
drifting like little eyes
on the glass in your hand

say: *pour it up*
        another round
another one

(wound) like a herringbone
chain around your neck.
        If you're gonna go, go wild.

If you're gonna sin, sin
in velvet, legs shaking on
the ceiling. Wherever you

place your   regrets
        is a worry for the morning,
there's too much

liquor to mourn anything.
Your mouth dances at the
        thought   of it, yes

liquor
like the Balm   in Gilead
you find a heaven each time

you open
your
mouth.

—

Are you capable of loving
anything   more than
you love   this   pill

dancing on the roof
                of your mouth:
catacomb of want, silly with

daydream and red wine.
You're laughing. The world
has gone   black, and you're

          laughing? Visible as
a cold sore, you crawl through
the house on all fours, giggling.

There are people who know
nothing about you, but   this:
she loves her drink   through

grim smiles, knitted brows
like dooming caterpillars.
          You laugh.

—

Everyday you take a vacation
          far away from a life
that haunts you. Your ribcage

haunts you, long having given up
solid food for liquid courage.
The visage of your skull   haunts

you, that's the truth.   You chortle
through. Lift a glass, say   *Amen*
where you meant   *Cheers*

You mean to cherish
every ounce of this
like it's the last.

It is far from the last.
You are such a   perfect
portrayal of suffering, you can

taste it, waylaid by the
          boundless dripping of
another broken glass.

—

Red, wound me!
You want to be colored
something you can   *imagine.*

You want to be a
vessel of   red will
you will   pay

it back.
Tenfold.
Tenfold.

Red ring around your
          mouth. The muscle lax.
You swallow to be born:

so, you are born.
"Bitter fruit,
make me good."

Diet Coke Sonnet

It can take time to do anything good.
I'm cutting down sugar, watching my carbs,
trying not to remember the cool press
of the scale beneath my feet. My best friend
says she likes Diet Coke, so I drink it
too. Lots of ice in a plastic cup, fizz
anoints my tongue like a bath bomb. The faint
taste of caramel colors everything.

When I was young, it was always more, more
more. I couldn't get enough of ruin.
My teeth could have rotted right out of my
damn head. It was an ugly scene. Sober,
I make amends first to my mouth, then to
the rest of me, parts gone soft, overripe.

Adolescence I
After Rita Dove

Picture the cage again: that was being
a girl. All night long, howling. Waiting
for someone to jangle the lock as a tease.

Mom said that my tears meant nothing
to everyone, so I learned to lick the salt
in silence, to paw at the bars, rouse moon

light. I used to think "anodyne" was like
Aphrodite, and meant beautiful. I used to
think about how language can

mold. I learned to make a body
from nothing but razorblades and fire. It was all
I knew, stripping skin from flesh.

And where it hissed, I rattled, gnashed.
Until the milky white cast of the moon
came to me in a cup and I drank it down.

Call it what you want: elixir, poison, sedative.
I learned it is anodyne, it is *beautiful*
to kiss your enemy with a mouth full of light.

Scorpio Rising

I was born early in the morning. They worried
about my brain for months after, placed nodes
on my skull to track its steady development.
When the tests came back normal, everyone
sighed with relief. Now, my brow furrows with
worry for my little self. Underweight, poked and
prodded, still slick with afterbirth. Then, after
adoption, I didn't speak. They worried twice.
Took me into a room for more tests. Everything
normal again, they never stopped to ask me why.
I just didn't have anything to say. Looking over
the paperwork of my birth, I redo my astrological
chart and find that I am a Scorpio rising. Ruled by
the planet Mars, motivated by truth. Patient.
Persistent. I didn't have anything to say,
most days, still don't, and sit in my own comfortable
silence. I'm motivated first by wonder. On bad days,
I ask, "Are you looking up?" I ask myself where
the moon is right now, where Mars roves, red
as a pomegranate. And you might call it foolish, but
the stars enchant. The stars coax a little heaven from
every ordinary moment, from the mind's pink slip.

What Has Placed Its Hand on Your Skin?

I have done all of this because I'm desperate for your touch.
Even a hurt animal will bend into touch.

Mother, lay your hand on me.
All centers of my body are begging for touch.

My heart, where it has grown petrified,
a heavy load for muscle, a touch

too much for its careful strings. What we learn
from our mothers is how we want someone to touch

us. How gentleness can soothe the unmoored.
My mind, after all these years, understands how touch-

ing it is to see a pink sky. The whole swallow of the trees
holding each other. What we ask of touch

is to be made. Oh mother, I want your common love.
A simple nod of knowing. Would you be touch-

ed by the vision of my face? Here are my hands, here are
the fronds of my eyelids. So much of me you can touch

and not disappear. Linger on my nose, tell me it is yours.
Mother, here are my feet, they have had to touch

the generous soil, painted red by its mud
where water and earth have come to touch.

All of this to bring you into my poem.
My grief extending a thousand miles only to touch

the hem of your dress. Even a hurt animal.
I misremember myself in the absence of touch.

Don't name it. I know the answers.
The fit of the truth, its callous touch.

Pushups

My whole god is a flight of good
gin. A mouth of florid speak,
the bite of a seed, tone.

While you do your humble work
I am a parable on time.
I am the hook of bitters, heady

on light and the concentration
it takes to become a pin-drop
of fluid. Flushed berry, the girth and menace

of a spider, toiling until
the color floods out and I become
everything you love. While you relax

your smooth muscle I am doing pushups
in the corner, waiting to topple you
like a wave from the ocean floor.

The fixed nebula of my desire:
what it wants is your throat, the gloss
of your eyes, its own planet.

I am all heel and mountain.
Shivered and hound, your greatest
adversary. I grow muscle where

your muscle grows quiet. Of better
days, there are none. There is only
me, the looking glass and the vision

beyond it. So delicate is our dance.
Carrying flowers on the tongue.
Oh how the ice age of your heart

found its warmth here. The spice
of liquorice root, your ever-coming
toward the strange familiar.

Will you recall the pop of citrus,
cardamom, the rude curve of your lips
as they form around one sip?

Innocent Enough

On Saturday, I buy a new brand of sparkling water.
Yuzu elderflower. The taste of the yuzu is strong,
spirited and fruity. It makes up for the almost clinical
taste of the elderflower. I drink sparkling water because

I want to drink alcohol. I want to drink alcohol because
it turns the haunt gossamer. Everything that colors me,
all at once, becomes smoke, moving away from my body
in somersaults, intoxicated twirls. This I inherit

from my mother. The desire for poison, to become vapor.
I can't help but think of her now, how she built me,
cell by cell in her body. Passing down her most deadly
traits, leaving the room as if neither of us had been

born there. I drink the sparkling water, relishing
the bright tang of the yuzu. Now, all my wants
are innocent enough. I want a cat, fruity drinks,
for someone to listen to me, a kiss.

I want to be adored for every lost day of my life,
a pair of lips touching the skin over my collarbone.

Go Ask ()

Sober oldheads call it
"dry-drunk"
my coffee too heavy with
creamer, sugar coating

my tongue   like fur.
To be sober is   to live
inside the echo,
hear yourself   once
            twice
                    three times for

good measure. The overly-sugared
coffee has ruined my day
I wanted to start it off   right

for there to be no dog shit
in the yard. For my packages
            to come on time,
for some woman to   love
            me

with her whole heart.
I've been lying to my therapist

            I don't get out for walks.
What we won't call agoraphobia
has left me stuttering

in the pantry. Nine cans of the same
kind of beans that I keep buying and
forgetting that I   bought them.

What have I got but   a surplus
of beans and desire   so thick

I can't stand it?

()

What kind of woman lies
        in therapy?

What does it say about me
that I adopted a dog and   gave
        him back because   I hated his
beauty, his

        eyes reminding me of
someone I once loved more than I loved
myself.   When given the opportunity

        I'll lose myself in just about anything.

Being the charming drunk at parties
led me to a bridge
                        where I wept
                        for what felt like
hours, didn't jump

because I couldn't ruin some
commuter's life.

Love, God, beans,   *please*
anything?

        take me away from the burden
that is me.   Disabuse me of the notion.

Directionless, I turn to novels about loss.
I masturbate on the highest setting
until I bleed.

God, if you'd   have me

()

Sometimes all it takes is for
the sun to hit your face,   you
can feel new with   only that.
Only warmth and gold light
like coins gleaming in
          an old cartoon.

It is only in this light
          that I am rich.

Sober   oldheads call that
Good
Orderly
Direction.

I call it a reason
          to keep going
despite debt and lonesome
so wrought it forces a knot
in   my throat.

The thing is
I *need* to be good.
          I spent too much time
worrying my friends,   taking their
money for drink.

And yes, they have forgiven me,
yes, I haven't had a drink in six years.
I'm better than I've ever been   but

            I have to be better than this.

God, can I be better than this?

                    who are you
                            if not trying
to be better than this?

God, if I am not golden yet
            can I be   bronze?
Tell me,   please   can I still

glisten?

Ouroboros II

I come back to my mother like the hand
of a clock moves back to 12. Every hour just
a means of traveling toward her. My mother
rules every century I live in, I press her name
into a glass, and each letter meets the plush
of my fingertips. In this way only, she never left me.
I lay claim to her by speaking her name.
I wasn't in need of sorrow, but it came.

○

I wasn't in need of sorrow, but it came. Heavy
as a moonless night, my brow furrowed under dark.
She could be dead, she could be eons away. I could
be 18, could be 32. It didn't matter, I traveled.
My heart slowed, my hands shook like butterflies.
They tell you your mother's name then expect you
not to wonder. I wandered in the night until I came
to her door. I was always walking toward her door.

○

I was always walking toward her door,
devotion the seed that sprouts in me, comes
vivid green. You can take and take and take from
the garden, but what happens when the soil grows
fangs, bites back? To bite as in to make a toothy meal
of the hand, bite like a measure of space. The space
she made within me has grown incisors. Fanged, it strikes.
Because blood is the answer to everything. Blood answers.

BABY GIRL W—

I've had three names, none of them very good.
I was born to be this manic, this many selves
lined up back-to-back like trading cards.
Any kind of love would have been fine for me,
yet I was born to the state more times than I'd like.
Baby Girl W—. I know it's merely a moniker
for the records, but I find tenderness in it anyway:
baby girl. As if, at some point, I was adored.
After some time, I've forgotten the names of my
foster parents. I remember their smiles, birthday
cards every year. Their hope for my life so great
it exceeded my tiny body. It seems common now,
but I use "I" too much in my poems. I would like
to divorce myself from the narrative. But I can't
stop thinking about *baby girl*, a toothsome thing.
I believe I was born to write a thousand poems about
my mother's lean brown hands, her keen eyelashes,
her name a lemon-drop stuck in the fold of my cheek.

Adolescence II
After Rita Dove

When Desirae learns I'm gay, she says
"I'm not, but I admire you for being out,
you're brave." Later, when she kisses me
in the hall in front of so many eyes,
I never feel braver. But it means nothing
to her, or her boyfriend with the stupid
name. That night, my eyelashes wet and
clinging to my cheeks like feathers. I think
What of bravery? It doesn't make a difference.
Being braver than the one you love is a curse,
when they can't love you, when they
hurt you to save themselves, what do you have
except for bravery? Not comfort, not
the warmth of love like a hand on your back.

Drunk

I waited my whole life to find sweetness
and only found it in a Cabernet Sauvignon.
You can imagine that saying goodbye was
bitter. My last drink: wine gone to vinegar.

The jig is up! I shouted to an empty
kitchen, the harsh yellow lights
made me look frenzied, electric. The tiles
on the floor began to curl up like fingers.

I shook and ate sugar for weeks. The life
of a drunk is a thief's life. You steal time,
steal from your loved ones. You break
and break again the good image of yourself.

In the absence of pills and poisons,
I was, first, a madwoman. Then, a saint
in my own eyes. Now, merely a woman
with time dripping from her hands.

the birthmother has expressive eyes

does the moment call for pause?
does the sentence allow for conjecture?
does the birthmother wish to speak in quietude?
does the act of being expressive, or having expressed,
mean that beyond the eyes, there was perhaps a light,
say, a revelation? and if so, is that revelation in relation
to the child who has many names, even within
this document? are the names here enclosed
an expression of the will of the state? or, perhaps,
the foster parents, deemed fit by said state?
and will the child have those same expressive eyes?
does she have them now? would the court permit us
to look into her eyes, just this once? and can we say
expressiveness is a trait, passed down through genetics,
easy to behold as a nose or high cheekbones?
what have we come here to do today?
separate a child from her mother.
write it down. describe the birthmother as tall,
slight, with grey hair, brown skin, her eyes.

To Unlearn the Narrative of the Dog

In the movie, Peter Pan chases his shadow
around the room. Tumbling and falling
over furniture, he catches it by its toe.

It's Wendy that takes his shadow and sews it
to his shoes with needle and thread. Secured,
Peter admires it stretched before him

on a nearby wall. His legs lean and long, toes
pointed like a ballerina. With Tinkerbell
stuck in a drawer, he promises Neverland.

You can chase yourself like a dog would,
like a fairy boy in tights. You can grow
slick with sweat, tire, trip over yourself,

get red in the face, red as an heirloom.
You can shake yourself out of silliness
when you catch you, loose the wreckage.

What happened to me is not extraordinary,
but it meant something. I had to stand still
long enough to sew the pieces back together.

I bled, it was no small task. I yelped each time
the needle pierced my skin. I left no gaps, not
for my mother, and reader, not even for you.

Harper

On her birthday, my niece sighs:
"Aunt Dani, am I dreaming?"
I say, "No, you're awake!" and she says,
"So that means you're really here!?"
Sometimes I wake up thinking nobody
loves me. Abandoned, abandoned,
here's a song: my niece laughing at
the dog rubbing its butt against me,
nipping at my toes. My niece sighing
as I feed her dinosaur chicken nuggets.
My niece explaining each and every
intricacy of her little, animated world.
My niece, my niece. Her name a blessing in
furs. Harper, *Harper*, dripping gold gold gold.

Calamity Suite

I.

For the sixth year in a row, I avoid relapse,
that damned thorned thing. I say "avoid"
because it is always a companion. When I was
23 and trying, it came to me week after week,

even when I promised my girlfriend
that I wouldn't. Some amber liquid in a glass held
weight. In my hand, the swallow living
in my throat. Relapse was a certain calamity. I tried

and tried but could not imagine. A failure
of the imagination can be a death sentence.
This is not hyperbole. I couldn't imagine.
When I closed my eyes, the room swayed.

II.

Be your own hero or get right with the end.
Let God enter you or close the door. I was through
with closed doors. I fought to open myself
to grace, and grace, many legged, shone through me.
Let God enter you or close the door. I've been in rooms
where dust danced in the light. So I danced in the light.

III.

Sometimes you cry out for your mother in the dim
light of the bathroom, your arms around a porcelain
bowl. Gut sick, sweat drenched, you lean into image,
on your knees, framed, a damsel. Everyone wants
to be saved. But no one else is coming. Get up off
the tile and wipe your mouth. Drink a glass of water.

IV.

The corner tenet of my sobriety is forgiveness
for myself. I know that I was no good, back then,
giving hell to my friends like a Christmas gift,
needing so much, always needing. When I stop

to ask the image of myself: *what is wrong with you?*
She says: *everything wrong with you.* I spent my best
years hiding behind a glass. I thought no one could
see me, but everyone could see me. Some of them

dared ask me to stop. I can't help but shift
in my seat when I think of it. How I laughed in their
faces, how I drank and drank and still did not
come to reach the bottom of my desire for more.

V.

I want to make mulberry wine. Instead I pick them
off of the bush, take them home to wash, and eat
each one raw. I get stained by temptation, but I don't
give in. It is enough to eat something sweet,
to let the tart notes pucker my lips into a passionate
kiss. I'm allowed to love these small things, my little
delights. My life now—soft as a petal unfurling.

Please Tell Me a Story of Mothers and Mothers and Mothers

What can be done with my
immortal need? Desperate,
clinging like sugar to a tooth,
a reflection hung in a mirror.

Like a lot of people, I was born.
Many moons later, I learned
my mother's name. I was told
"You can be afraid, but you can't

be greedy." I was greedy anyway,
could not ration my want. I loved
with so much fervor, I vibrated.
The day mom stormed into

my room and dropped her name.
Sarah. I turned it into a prayer.
I put my back toward the door and
wrote her name in cursive all over

the page. Bleeding all over the stark
white of the page. For days, I sang.
It was all I could do, even now,
the many times I have written

"Sarah," called her "mother"
though she would probably shirk
the name. The thing about mothers
is they can't get away with absence.

We let fathers disappear, miss recitals,
forget their children's middle names,
let fathers be "dead beat"—a violence
in the phrase. Even now, my own father

absent from the page. His music ringing
through my fingers. His rights
terminated "involuntarily."
His nose perhaps even mine.

Everyone wants a perfect mother,
and I am no different.
In session, I tell my therapist
"If she had just gotten sober, got

her shit together, my life wouldn't
be like this!" See, laying blame like
one foot after another. With all I
am, all I know, she still can't

escape my judgment. My friends
who gave me money for liquor,
who watched wet-eyed as I
descended, they would say

the same about me, my living.
These days, I'm not trying to
hurl myself off a bridge, or cutting
my wrists to the pink meat.

In a lot of ways, my first language
was harm. I blame my mother
for that, for the way fists molded
the bends of my fat body.

I can blame my mother for a lot
of things, but I can't blame her
for the way I blame her. That's all me.
I survived so much and still couldn't

tell you what is and isn't my fault.
Do you understand what I mean?
What can be done with a mother
I didn't know but tell my story?

Held steadfast to a tale that
doesn't leave room for breathing.
The air in my lungs stalled, and
can't come out. Like the day

I left my friend's apartment
not knowing where
I was going to sleep that night.
I couldn't *breathe*. Functionally,

could not air in, air out. A lock
on my chest. I stumbled most of
the way down a long flight of steps.
I could find a way to blame

my mother for this too.
For the way I still found the means
to get high in a stranger's basement.
Nothing is fair about my lonely.

My problem with my mother
is that she died. And when I
looked for her, she was
a myth. In therapy I say I want

to forgive her, to be forgiven.
Like a child in the kitchen
saying grace, I bow my head.
Sarah, if I am pure, please

Notes

"Sarah W–" borrows lines from "The Shampoo" by Elizabeth
   Bishop.

The "Go Ask..." poems are inspired by the novella "Go Ask
   Alice."

"Search Engine Results" was inspired by "Wishbone" by
   Richard Silken, particularly the lines "My adoptive mother/
   did not love me in a way I could understand, so I learned to
   live/ in the hollow."

"Abandoned, Abandoned, Let Me Sing My Song" includes
   the title of Rose Royce's song "Love Don't Live Here
   Anymore."

"A Colonial Project" includes facts about adoption in South
   Korea and China found in NPR stories written by Deann
   Borshay Liem and Emily Feng respectively.

"You've Got an Enemy in Pennsylvania" comes from a tee shirt
   design by Philadelphia-based artist Ghost Bongo.

"Adoptee Log #4" includes a quote from the Jeanette
   Winterson memoir, *Why Be Happy When You Could Be
   Normal?*

"the birthmother has expressive eyes" takes its language from
   my birth history, provided by The Children's Home of
   Pittsburgh.

Thanks

Many thanks to the editorial team at Sundress Publications, with gratitude to Krista Cox, my editor, for making this process so seamless and wonderful.

This book is dedicated to my brothers David and Dakota, who are also adopted, for inspiring me to revisit my search. My best friends and biggest champions, I love you both so much.

To Shanai, for sticking beside me the past 20 years.

My love to the Poet Data Team, Cale Davis and Diehl Edwards, for all those early mornings spent in meditation with you.

Thank you to Rosebud Ben-Oni and Brittany Hailer for guiding me through the multiple iterations of this manuscript.

I owe a debt of gratitude to Liana Maneese, Kim Rooney, my press mates Kay E. Bancroft, SG Huerta, and Abigail Raley, and the editors that published individual works from this book.

Thank you to my sober community in Pittsburgh, South Carolina, and beyond.

Love and thanks to Toi Derricotte, the one poet I am always trying to impress.

Finally, thank you to Sarah, who taught me to love with my whole heart what my eyes could not see.

About the Author

Dani Janae is a poet and journalist from Pittsburgh, Pennsylvania. Her work has been published by *Longleaf Review, SWWIM, RHINO Poetry, South Florida Poetry Journal,* and others. She lives in South Carolina.

Other Sundress Titles

Burns
SG Huerta
$17.95

Unrivered
Donna Vorreyer
$17.95

Pork Fluff
Tiffany Hsieh
$17.95

The Parachutist
Jose Hernandez Diaz
$16.00

Florence
Bess Cooley
$16.99

Back to Alabama
Valerie A. Smith
$16.00

Tales from Manila Ave.
Patrick Joseph Caoile
$21.95

Death Fluorescence
Julia Bouwsma
$20.95

Still My Father's Son
Nora Hikari
$17.95

Pure Fear, American Legend
Laura Dzubay
$20.00

Spoke the Dark Matter
Michelle Whittaker
$16.00

Good Son
Kyle Liang
$16.00

DANGEROUS BODIES / ANGER ODES
redwood, stevie
$16.00